GRADE ONE

MICHAEL AARON PIANO COURSE

LESSONS

Especially designed to create student interest and progress by combining basic elements of piano technic with melody

correlated material	begin with
THEORY (11001TH)	page 4
TECHNIC (11001TC)	page 8
PERFORMANCE (11001PF)	page 8

PREFACE

To express oneself musically, or play a musical instrument, is a normal desire inherent in most individuals. To encourage and stimulate that desire, this course was planned with two thoughts uppermost in mind, namely *Student Interest* and *Progress.* To quote a psychological axiom, "INTEREST is the mother of ATTENTION and ATTENTION is the mother of MEMORY." In order to sustain the interest of the student many pieces of melodic content are introduced. However, underlying each piece, is a basic principle of piano technic. Note Reading Games, Rhythm Patterns, Explanatory Charts, Technical Studies, Musical Dictionary, and many other features combine to give the student a thorough foundation. All the material in this course has been carefully graded and arranged in a logical and stepwise manner to lighten the task of both the student and teacher.

CONTENTS

Introduction to Music
Reference and Review

The Grand Staff

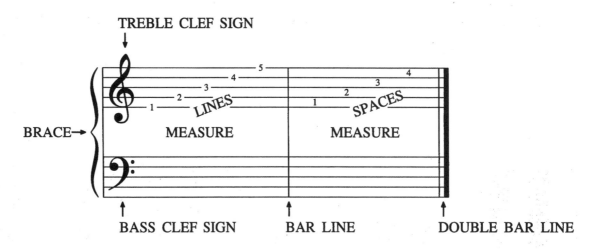

Note Values

Rest Values

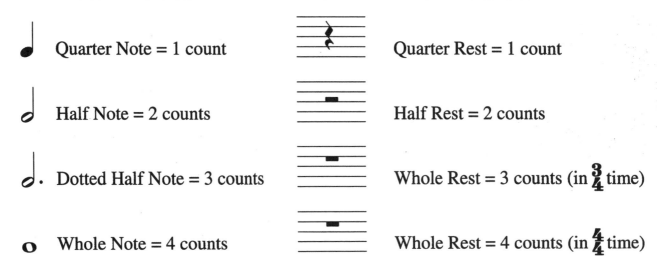

Time Signatures

The Scale

The Scale is the foundation upon which music is written. All melodies are composed of notes of a scale in various forms.

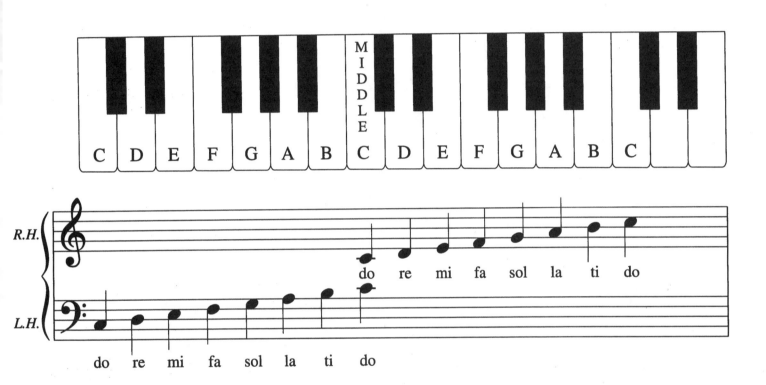

1. Play the scale in the upper staff (treble) with one finger of the right hand.

2. Now play the scale in the lower staff (bass) with one finger of the left hand.

3. Note the relationship to the keyboard, also the order: line note, space note, line note, etc.

Preparation for "First Lesson"

Place your fingers over the keys as shown in the drawing below and you will be in the correct position to play "First Lesson." Notice that both thumbs are placed on MIDDLE C.

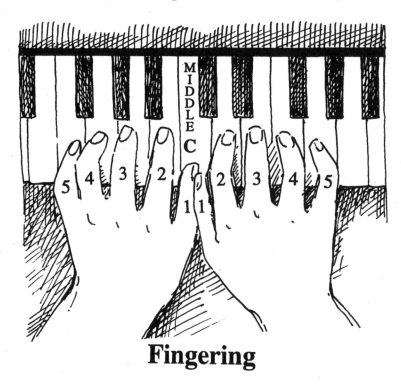

Fingering

In piano music, a number may be placed near a note to show you which finger to use.

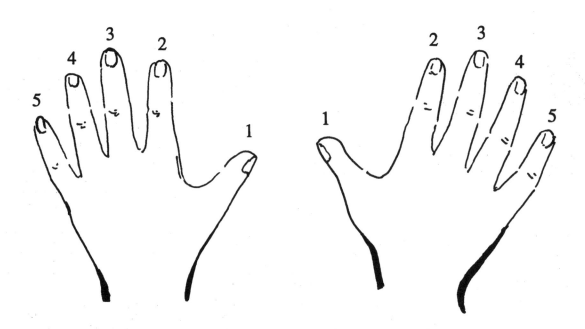

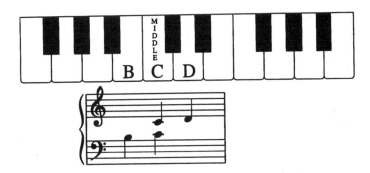

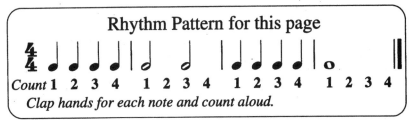

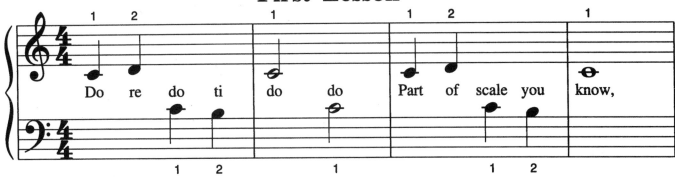

Rhythm Pattern for this page

Count 1 2 3 4 1 2 3 4 1 2 3 4 1 2 3 4

Clap hands for each note and count aloud.

First Lesson

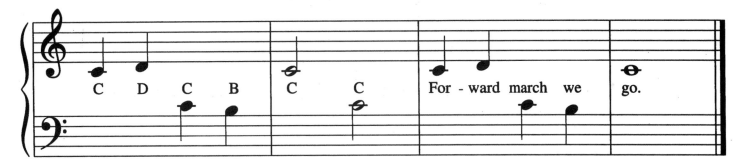

Do re do ti do do Part of scale you know,

C D C B C C For - ward march we go.

Up and Down

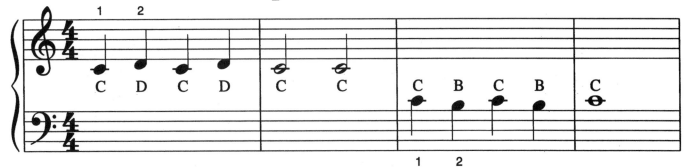

C D C D C C C B C B C

Up and down we trav - el, Hap - py as can be.

11001A

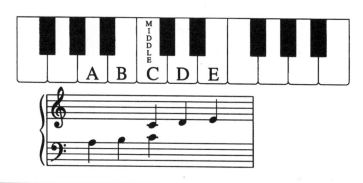

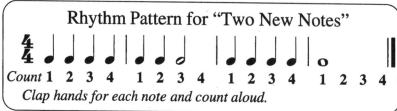

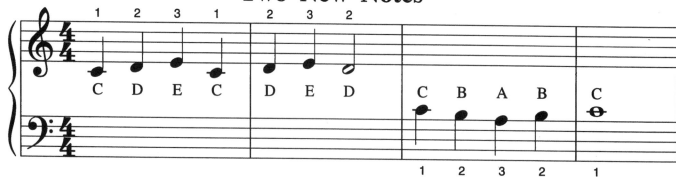

Rhythm Pattern for "Two New Notes"

Count 1 2 3 4 1 2 3 4 1 2 3 4 1 2 3 4

Clap hands for each note and count aloud.

Two New Notes

C D E C   D E D   C B A B   C

You have learned two   new notes here,   Name them please for   me.

Dancing Notes

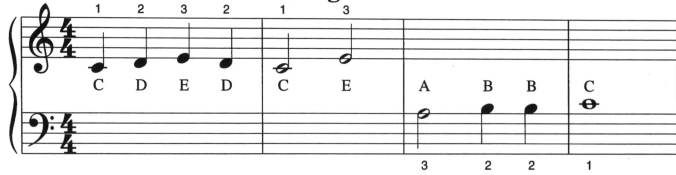

C D E D   C E   A B B   C

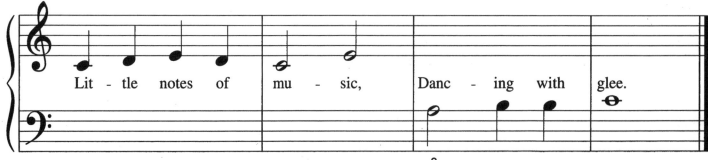

Lit - tle notes of   mu - sic,   Danc - ing with   glee.

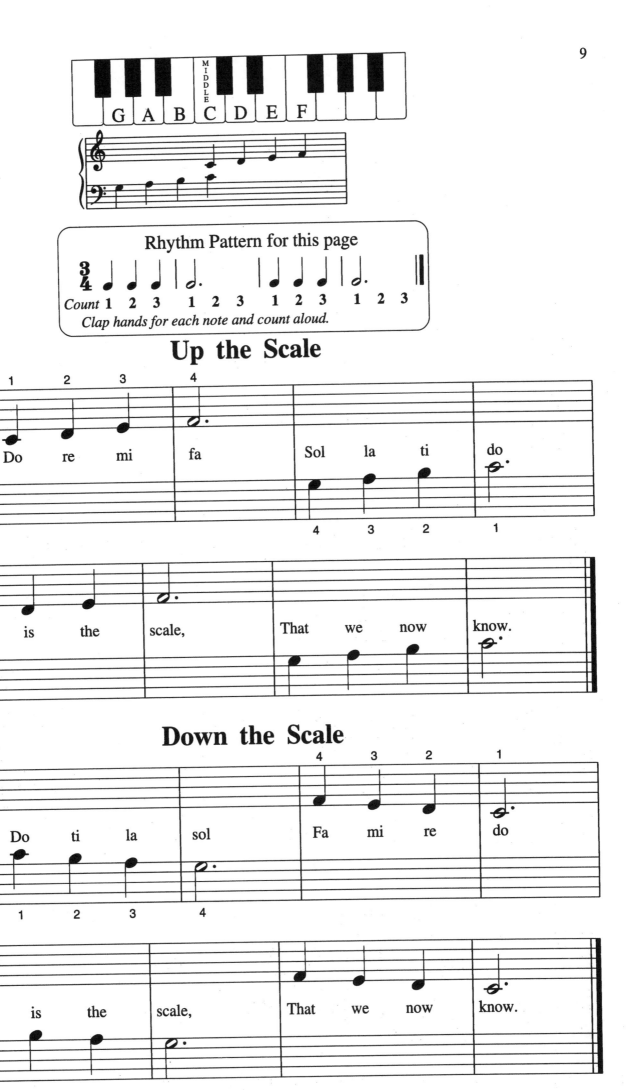

Rhythm Pattern for this page

Count **1 2 3 1 2 3 1 2 3 1 2 3**

Clap hands for each note and count aloud.

Up the Scale

1   2   3   4

Do   re   mi   fa   Sol   la   ti   do

4   3   2   1

It   is   the   scale,   That   we   now   know.

Down the Scale

4   3   2   1

Do   ti   la   sol   Fa   mi   re   do

1   2   3   4

It   is   the   scale,   That   we   now   know.

Ding Dong

Hark the bells are ring-ing, ring-ing, Ding dong, ding dong,

How they fill the eve-ning with their sweet, sweet song.

Diving

Note Reading Tests

Spell the words by writing the correct letter name of each note.
To complete each test play the correct notes on the piano.

Example

NAME OF WORD

NAME OF WORD

Ace

A   C   E

Work out the following tests in the same way.

NAME OF WORD

NAME OF WORD

NAME OF WORD

NAME OF WORD

NAME OF WORD

NAME OF WORD

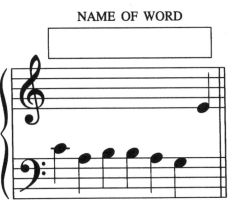

NAME OF WORD

NAME OF WORD

14

Progress

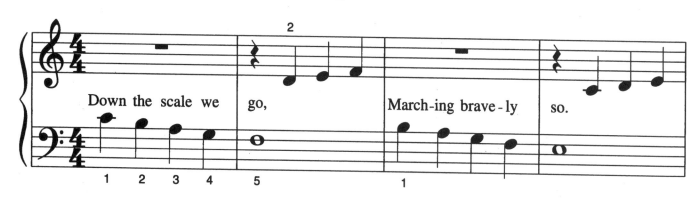

Prepare for "Sandman's Lullaby"

Place your fingers over the keys as shown in the drawing below and you will be in the correct position to play "Sandman's Lullaby."

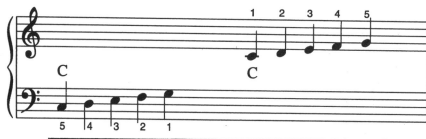

LEFT HAND 5 is on the C below Middle C.

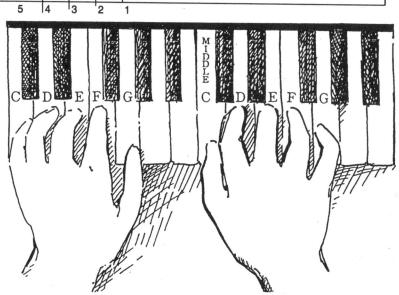

(This is a left hand note, even though the stem goes up.)

Slurs and Ties

The SLUR is a curved line over two or more notes of different pitch indicating that the notes are played legato. Legato means to play in a smooth and connected manner. ⌒ or ⌣

The TIE is also a curved line but connects two notes of the same pitch, indicating that the time value of the two notes is combined. The second note of the pair is counted and held but not played again. ⌒ or ⌣

Sandman's Lullaby

Moderato (*a medium rate of speed—not too fast*)

Sleep   my   ba - by,

Close   your   eyes,

Sand - man's   call - ing,

From   the   skies.

*p (softly)

*p is the symbol for the Italian word piano, which means soft.

11001A

Note Reading Tests

To complete each test play the correct notes on the piano.

NAME OF WORD

NAME OF WORD

NAME OF WORD

NAME OF WORD

NAME OF WORD

NAME OF WORD

NAME OF WORD

NAME OF WORD

Now SPELL the following words with the correct notes.

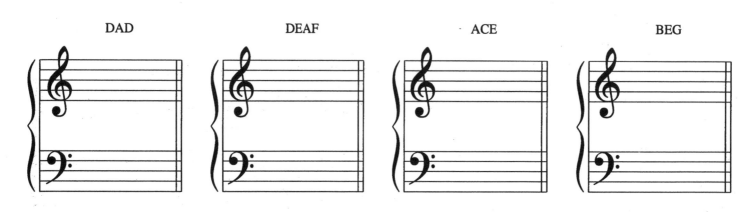

DAD

DEAF

ACE

BEG

Hands Together

Notice that in measure one each hand begins with finger 5, playing together. In measure two, each hand begins with finger 1, playing together.

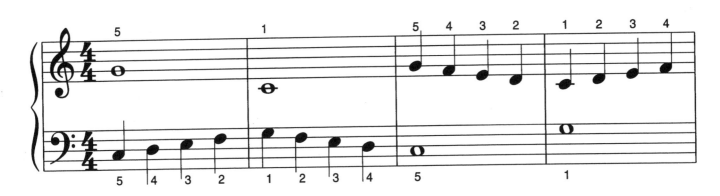

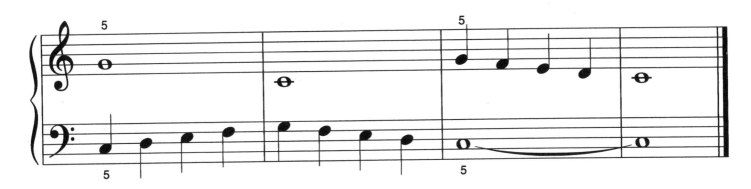

Our New Horn

18

The Swing

Moderato

Up in the sky, Ev - er so high,

Swing - ing so free in the air.

Up in the sky, Ev - er so high,

With - out a wor - ry or care.

Trill Study for Right Hand

TRILL: to alternate a note with the next one above, playing one right after the other.

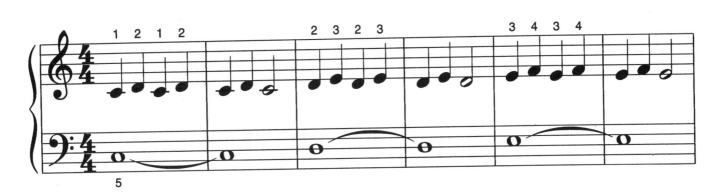

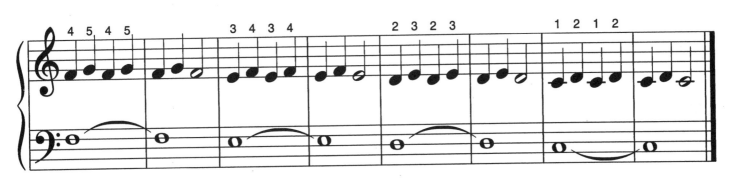

Trill Study for Left Hand

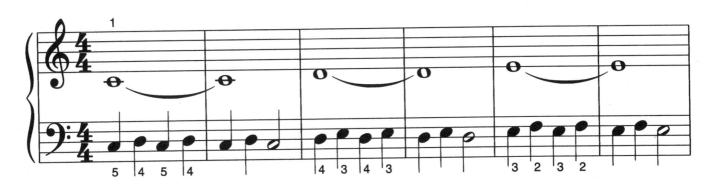

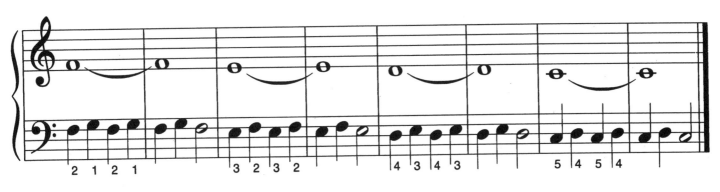

11001A

The Half Step

A HALF STEP or HALF TONE is the smallest difference in pitch (high or low) between two tones on the piano.

The Sharp Sign ♯

A SHARP placed before a note RAISES it a half step.

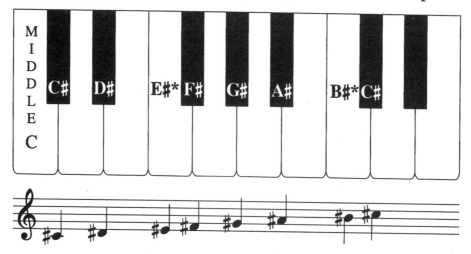

*E Sharp is played on the same white key as F.

*B Sharp is played on the same white key as C.

Sharpen Up!

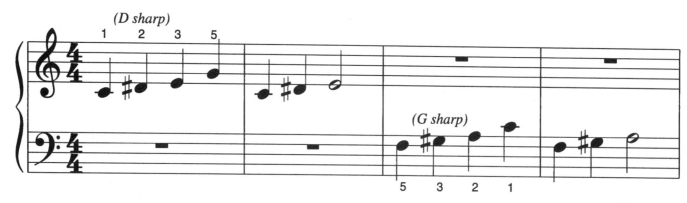

The Flat Sign ♭

A FLAT placed before a note LOWERS it a half step.

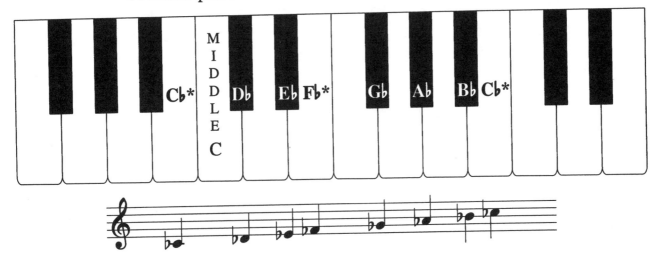

*C Flat is played on the same white key as B.

*F Flat is played on the same white key as E.

Flatten Out!

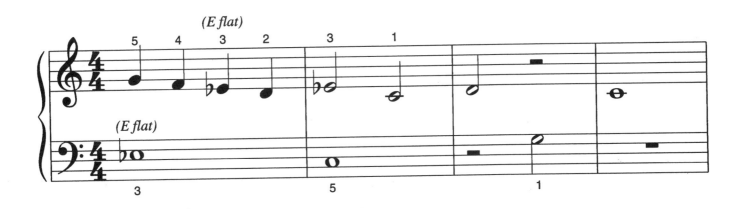

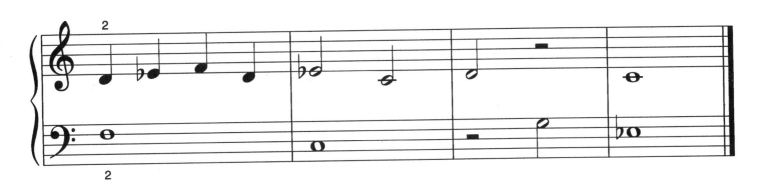

11001A

The Natural Sign ♮

A NATURAL before a note cancels any previous sharp or flat in the same measure.

EXAMPLE

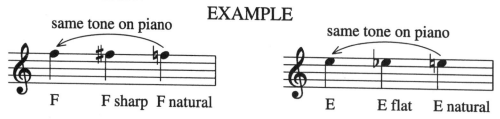

You're a Natural!

The Whole Step

A WHOLE STEP or WHOLE TONE is the same distance as TWO HALF STEPS. For example:

C to C♯ is a half step; C♯ to D is a half step. Therefore C to D is a whole step.

C♯ to D is a half step; D to D♯ is a half step. Therefore C♯ to D♯ is a whole step.

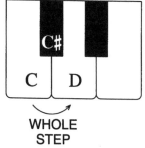

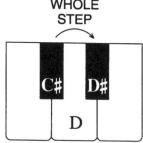

Major Scale Pattern

Every MAJOR SCALE is composed of WHOLE STEPS and HALF STEPS. Here is the order:

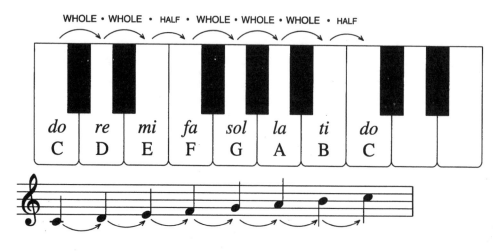

Hand Position for "Study in G"

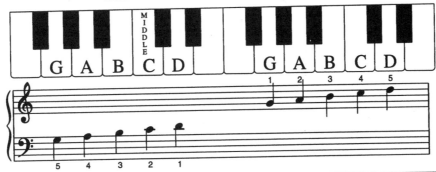

Key of G Major: The studies on this page are written in the Key of G Major. Notice the sharp (F♯) in the KEY SIGNATURE right after the Treble and Bass Clefs. If there were Fs in this piece, they would all be played F sharp.

Study in G

Slurs

Note Reading Tests

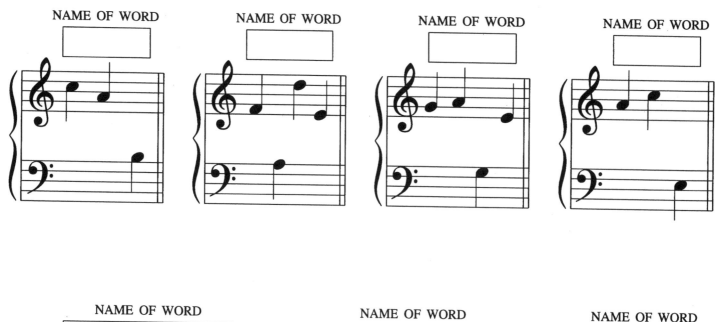

SPELL the following words with the correct notes.

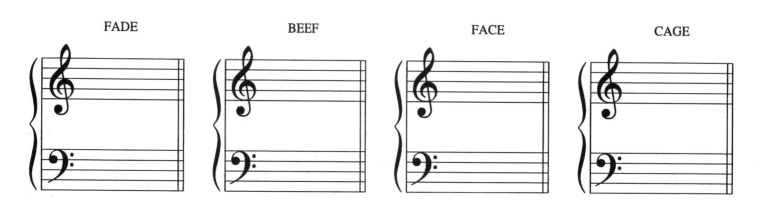

To complete each test play the correct notes on the piano.

The Old Mill Wheel

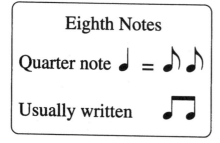

Follow the Leader
(Eighth Notes)

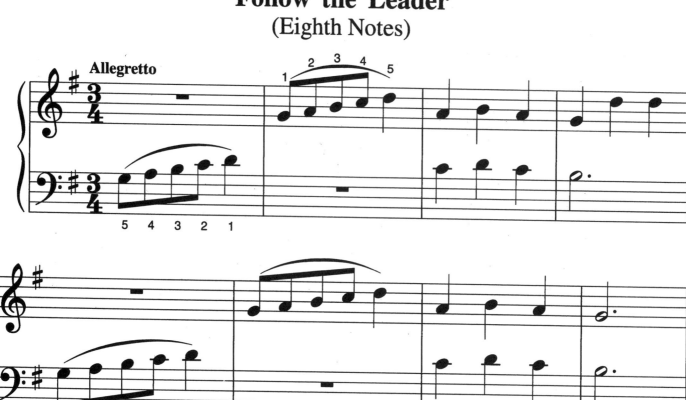

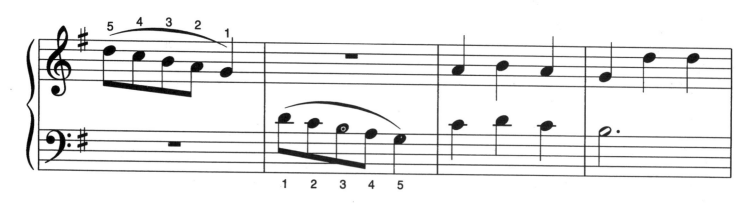

Dynamics Chart

Symbol	Term	Definition
pp	pianissimo	very soft
p	piano	soft
mp	mezzo piano	moderately soft
mf	mezzo forte	moderately loud
f	forte	loud
ff	fortissimo	very loud

Rhythm Pattern for "Hunting Song"*

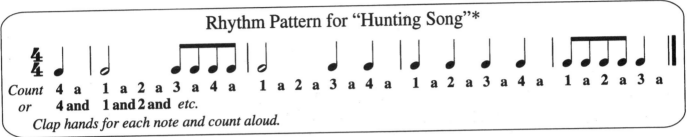

Count 4 a 1 a 2 a 3 a 4 a 1 a 2 a 3 a 4 a 1 a 2 a 3 a 4 a 1 a 2 a 3 a

or 4 and 1 and 2 and *etc.*

Clap hands for each note and count aloud.

Hunting Song

Allegro (Fast)

mf A - way thru the woods, Where the horn and hound are
call - ing A - way thru the woods, In the morn-ing fresh and
clear *f* A - way, *p* a - way *pp* far a - way.

*Notice that the first measure of this song begins on the FOURTH BEAT and the last measure ends on the THIRD BEAT. These two measures, although incomplete in themselves, equal one complete measure. The beginning note is called a "pick-up."

Transposition

In playing a song, it is sometimes necessary to change the key to a higher or lower one in order to suit the voice. This changing from one key to another is called TRANSPOSING.

TRANSPOSITION will also give the student more skills at the piano keyboard.

How to Transpose "Sandman's Lullaby" to Key of G

1. Place hands on five-finger position in G:

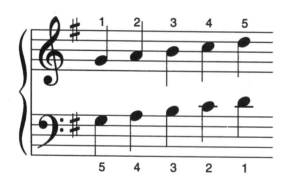

Reproduced from Page 15

2. Play right hand melody using same fingering:

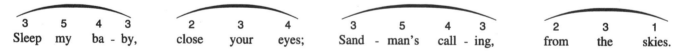

3. Play left hand accompaniment using same fingering:

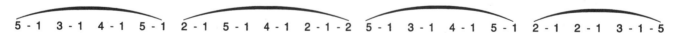

4. Play hands together.

Transpose "The Swing" (page 18) to the Key of G.

Correct Fingering

A good pianist must use the correct fingering. Correct fingering will make your playing much smoother. It will also help you to connect the melody and develop a good singing tone in piano playing.

Observe the correct fingering in "Boatsman Chant." In the sixth measure, the third finger of the right hand changes from E to F.

rit. ritardando (ritard.) – Gradually slower

𝄐 Fermata – Hold note longer than its actual value

Boatsman Chant

Canadian Folk Song

Andante *(Slowly)*

p Faint - ly as tolls the eve - ning chime, Our

voic - es keep tune, And our oars keep time, ___ Our

voic - es keep tune, And our oars keep ___ time.

rit.

Key of F Major: This piece is written in the Key of F Major. The flat (B♭) shown in the key signature means that all Bs are FLAT and played on BLACK KEYS.

Dotted Quarter Note

Quarter note ♩ = ♫ two eighth notes

Dotted quarter note ♩. = ♫♪ three eighths

The Busy Mill
(Study in Dotted Quarters)

Double Note Study (Intervals)
For Right Hand

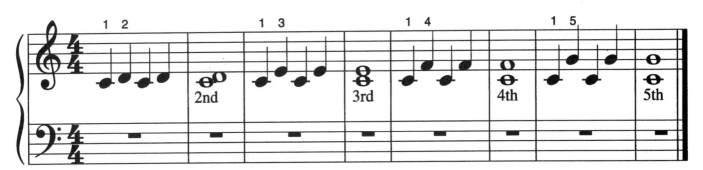

Double Note Study
For Left Hand

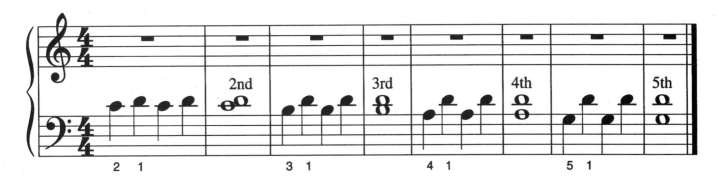

Music Hour

Have you played your mu - sic, mu - sic, mu - sic, Have you played your mu - sic here to - day?

Yes I played my mu - sic, mu - sic, mu - sic, And I like my mu - sic just this way.

Are You Sleeping?
(Round)

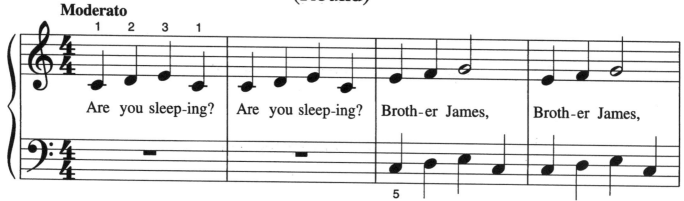

Prayer

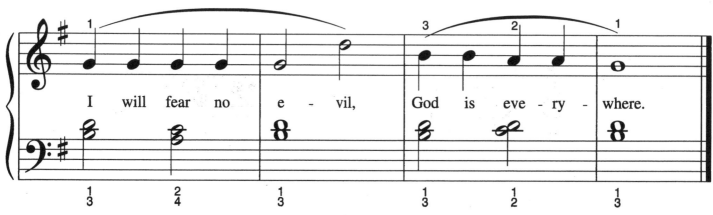

11001A

Triads

A triad is a chord composed of three tones formed in the following manner:

1. Play a succession of five tones in the scale.

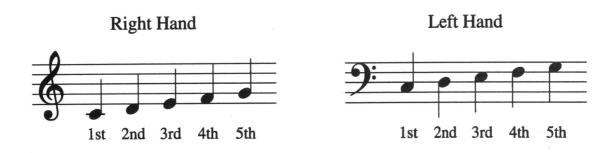

Right Hand

1st 2nd 3rd 4th 5th

Left Hand

1st 2nd 3rd 4th 5th

2. Omit 2nd and 4th tones.

1st 3rd 5th

1st 3rd 5th

3. Strike the three tones together on the piano.

— 5th
— 3rd
— Root

— 5th
— 3rd
— Root

Triads of the Major Scale

Form a triad on each note of the scale.

Play hands separately, then together.

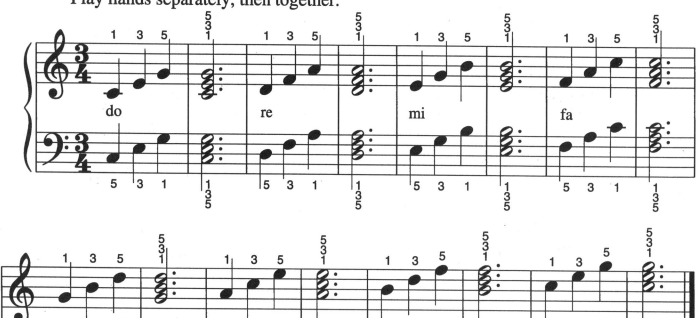

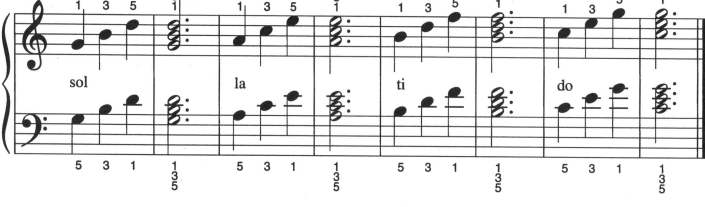

The Three Major Triads

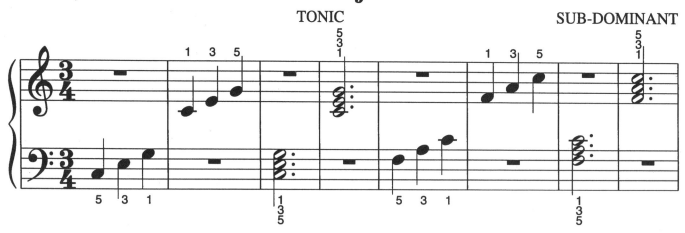

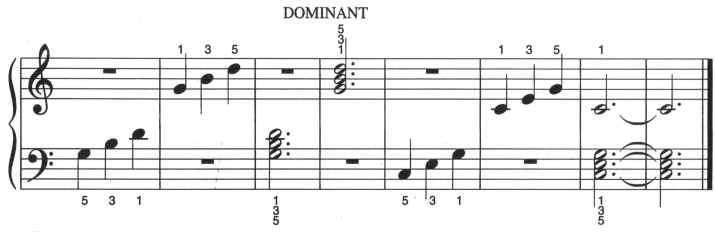

Evening Song
(Dotted Quarters)

Chord Study in C Major

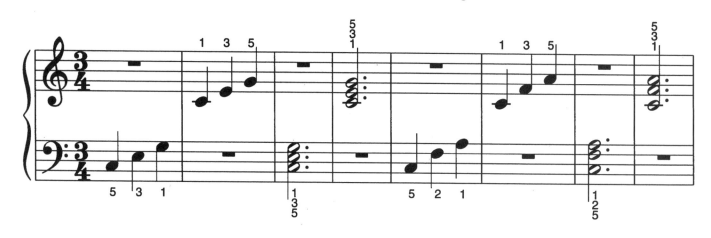

The Sunflower

Moderato

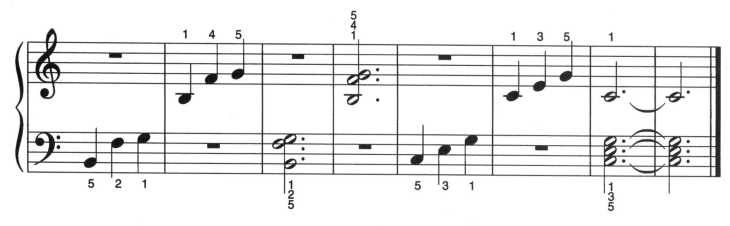

p Sun gold - en,   Rays stream - ing,   The world a - wak - ens,

My pet - als,   Un - fold - ing,   Re - flect thy light.

New Time Signature – $\frac{6}{8}$

6 – 6 counts in each measure

8 – ♪ (eighth note) gets one count

ɤ (eighth rest) also gets one count

In $\frac{6}{8}$ time a quarter note ♩ *gets two counts*

a dotted quarter note ♩. gets three counts

a dotted quarter rest 𝄽· also gets three counts

> Tap the rhythm before playing the following exercises.
> Accent the 1st and 4th beats of each measure.

In a Canoe

STACCATO, shown by a dot above or below a note, means to release that note quickly.

Study in Staccato

Accent each note and release key quickly. Play hands separately, then together.

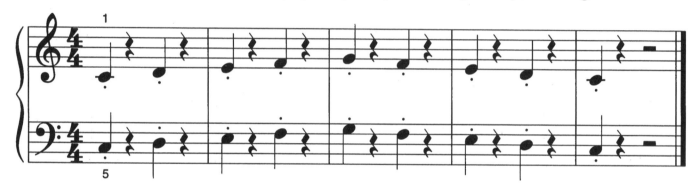

Banjo

Allegretto

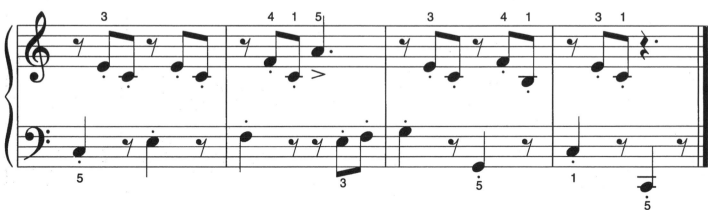

Dance of the Wooden Shoes

Allegretto con brio *(Quickly, with energy)*

Flemish Folk Tune

Note Reading Tests

NAME OF WORD

NAME OF WORD

NAME OF WORD

NAME OF WORD

NAME OF WORD

NAME OF WORD

NAME OF WORD

NAME OF WORD

Write letter names of lines and spaces in the treble and bass staffs.

LINES

SPACES

TREBLE

BASS

TREBLE

BASS

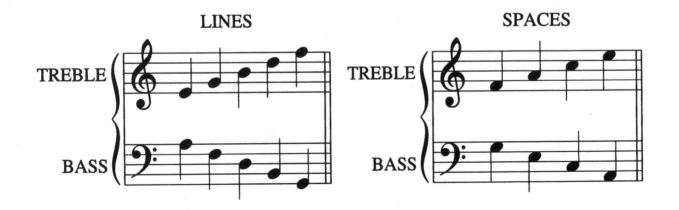

To complete each test play the correct notes on the piano.

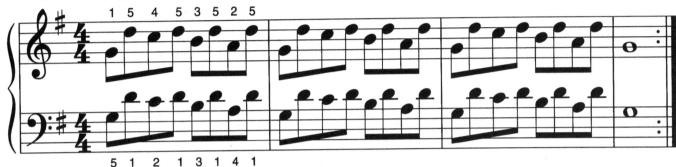

Repeat sign – Go back to the beginning and play the piece again.

Finger Study

Play hands separately, then together.

Spring Song

Folk Song

Moderato

mp Sing,　sing,　sing,　For to - day is Spring.

Flow - ers bloom-ing, Plants are grow-ing, Trees are green, Their leaves are show-ing;

Sing,　sing,　sing,　For to - day is Spring.

Rockin' On

dim. (diminuendo) – gradually getting softer

Chord Study in F Major

Wake Up!

At the Skating Rink

Key of G Major: This study is written in the Key of G Major. The sharp (F♯) shown in the key signature means that all Fs are SHARP and played on BLACK KEYS.

Chord Study in G Major

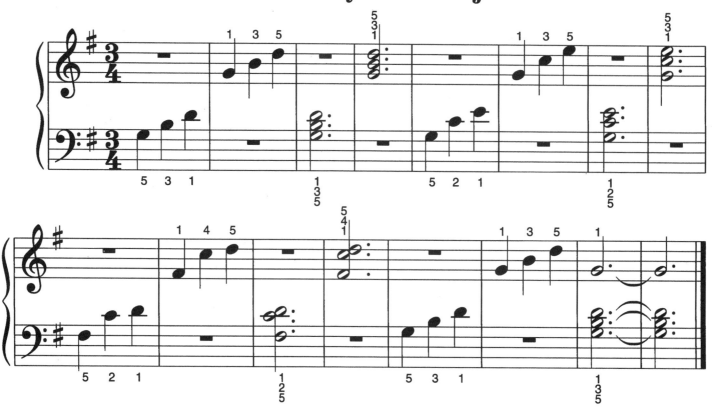

Fun in the Sun

*Look up all new terms and symbols in the "Dictionary of Musical Terms" on page 63.

11001A

The Birdling's Serenade

48

Key of D Major: This piece is written in the Key of D Major. The two sharps (F♯ and C♯) shown in the key signature mean that all Fs and Cs are SHARP and played on BLACK KEYS.

Evening Chimes

Moderato

Folk Song

Eve - ning chimes ring sweet - ly, so sweet - ly,

Eve - ning chimes, so peace - ful and clear.

Sun in the west, Time now to rest,

Eve - ning chimes, so peace - ful and clear.

Trill Study

To obtain a smooth and even effect, all eighth notes should match each other in length of sound.

Key of B Flat Major: This piece is written in the Key of B Flat Major. The two flats (B♭ and E♭) shown in the key signature mean that all Bs and Es are FLAT and played on BLACK KEYS.

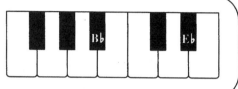

The Choir

*Look up all new terms and symbols in the "Dictionary of Musical Terms" on page 63.

11001A

Scale Study

In playing this Scale Study be sure that your thumb is relaxed.
This will help you to cross the thumb under the third finger.

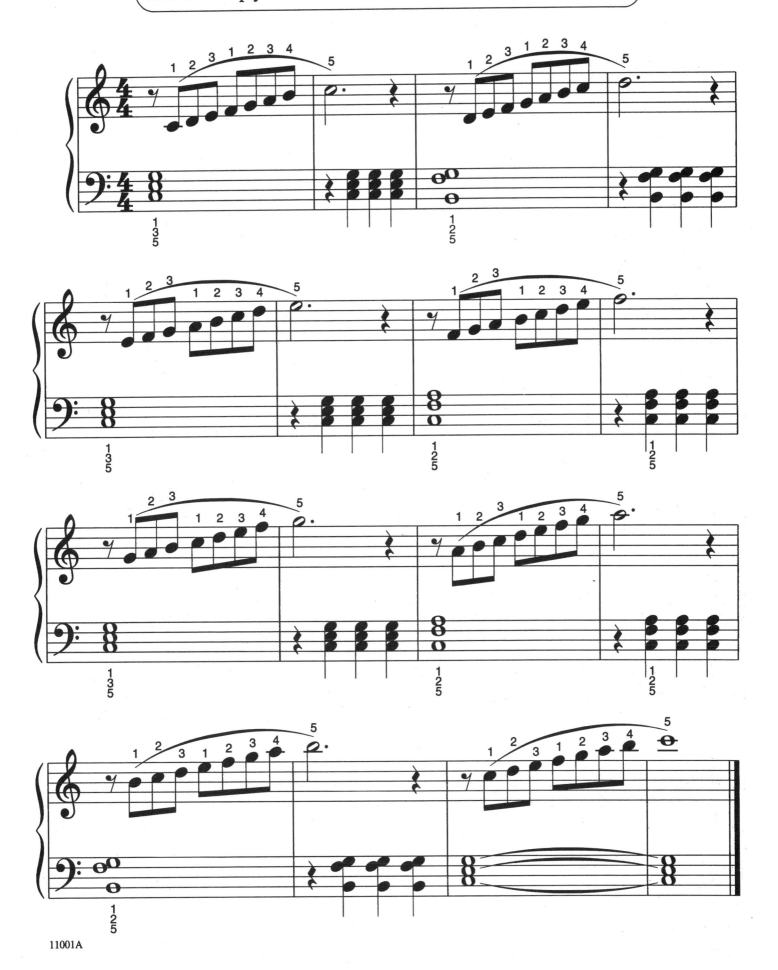

Key of A Major: This piece is written in the Key of A Major. The three sharps (F♯, C♯ and G♯) shown in the key signature mean that all Fs, Cs and Gs are SHARP and played on BLACK KEYS.

The Pied Piper

(This piece may be played an octave higher.)

Scale Study

The Singing Brook

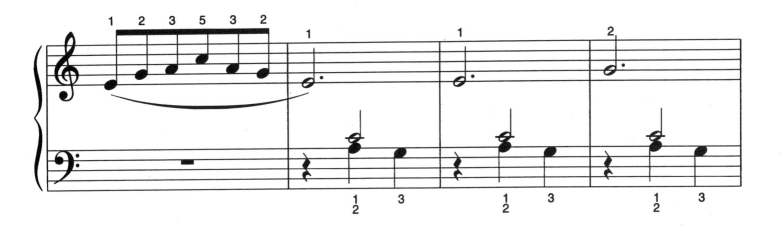

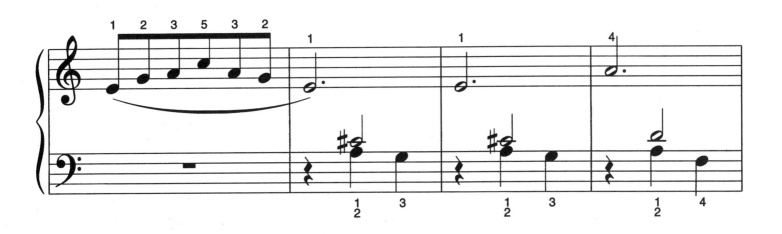

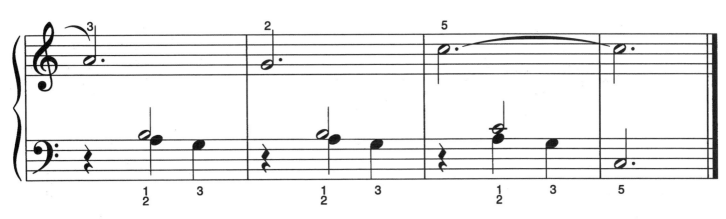

Key of E Flat Major (or C Minor): The three flats (B♭, E♭ and A♭) shown in the key signature mean that all Bs, Es and As are FLAT and played on BLACK KEYS. In this piece, note that the Bs are preceded by a NATURAL (♮) SIGN. This means the Bs are *not* to be flat.

Ghosts at Midnight
(Key of C Minor)

*Look up all new terms and symbols in the "Dictionary of Musical Terms" on page 63.

11001A

Drummer Boy

Allegretto

f Left, left, left, right, left, I'm the ar-my drum-mer boy, Beat-ing on my drum.

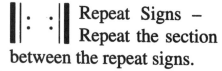

Repeat Signs – Repeat the section between the repeat signs.

Chopstick Revels

Allegretto

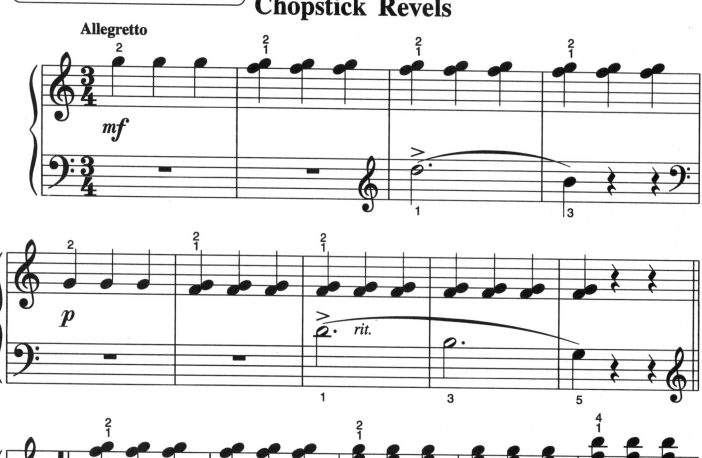

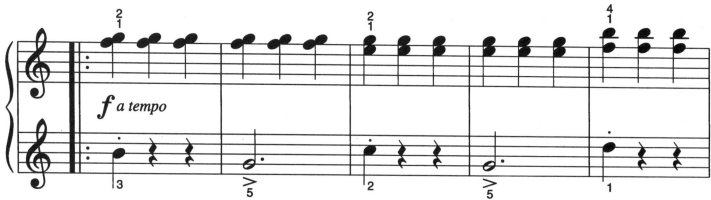

First ending – play first time only.   *Second ending – play second time.*

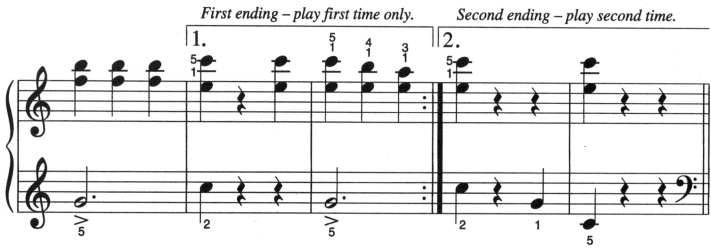

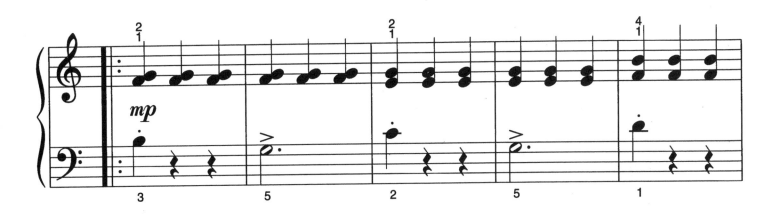

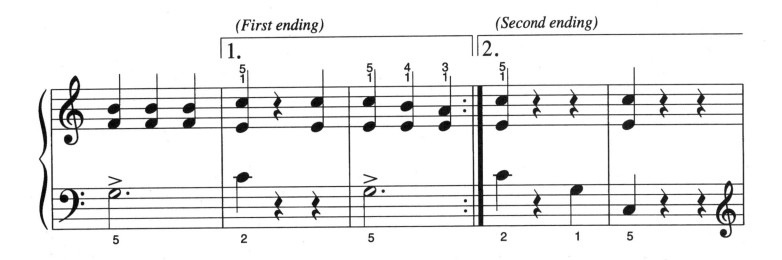

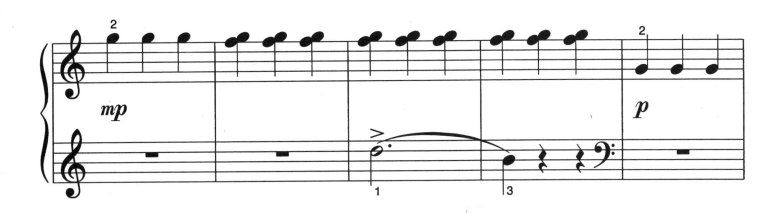

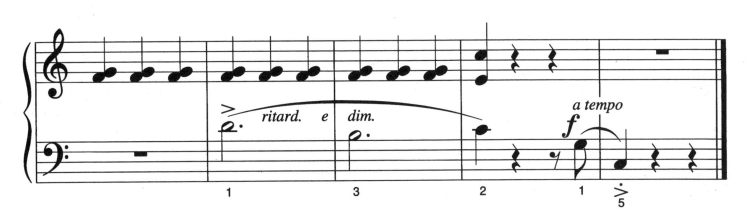

Jingle Bells

Allegretto

mf Jin - gle bells Jin - gle bells, Jin - gle all the way,

Oh what fun it is to ride, In a one horse o - pen sleigh _____

Jin - gle bells Jin - gle bells, Jin - gle all the way,

Oh what fun it is to ride in a one horse o - pen sleigh.

The Major Scales and Chords

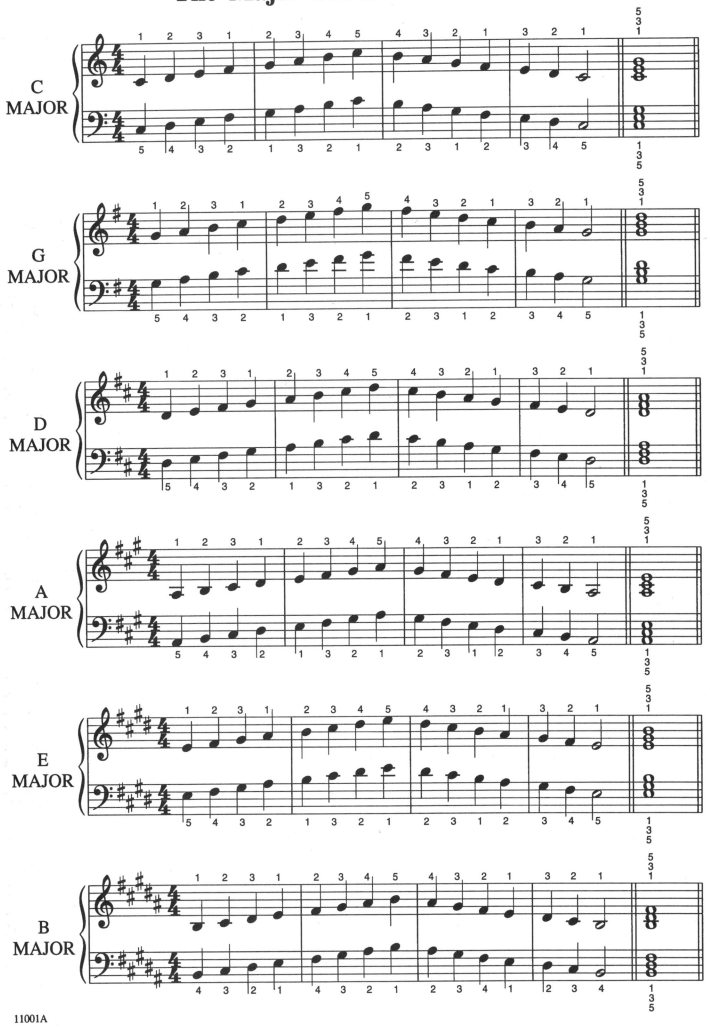

The Major Scales and Chords

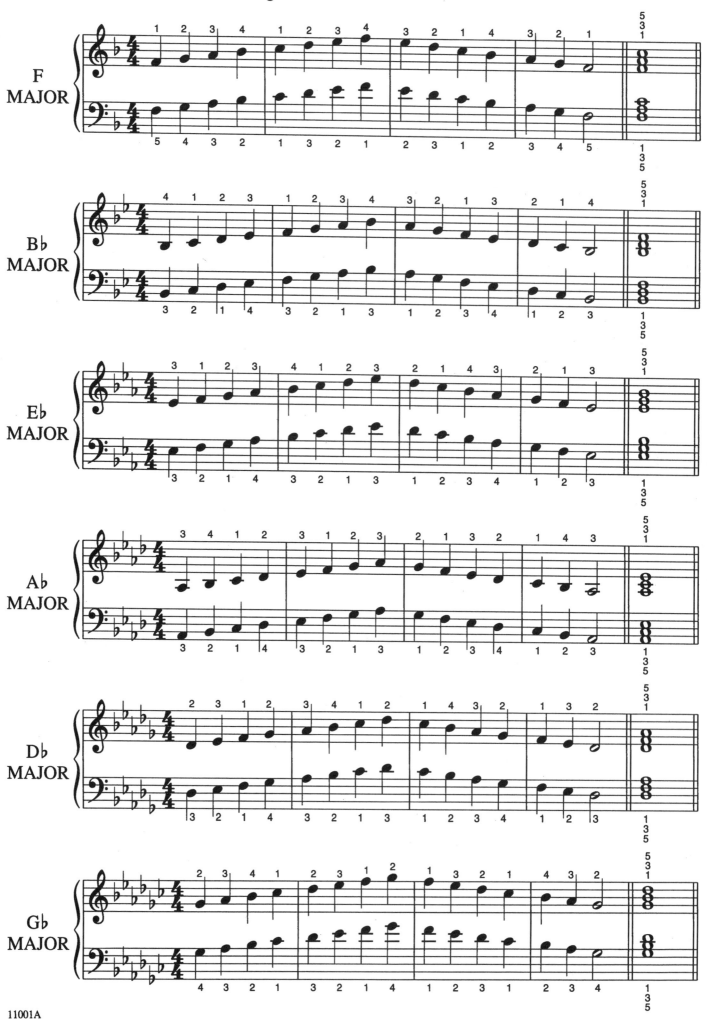

DICTIONARY OF MUSICAL TERMS

A Tempo ....Resume the original tempo

Accelerando ....Increase speed gradually

Accent mark........... > ....Play the note louder

Allegretto......................................Moderately fast tempo, lively

Allegro ....Fast, brisk tempo

Andante ....Slowly

Crescendo (cresc.) ⟨ ....Gradually getting louder

D.C. al Fine ....(Da Capo al Fine) Return to the beginning and play to the word "Fine"

Decrescendo (decresc.) ⟩.....Gradually getting softer

Diminuendo (dim.) ⟩.........Gradually getting softer

Fermata .... ⌢ ....Hold the note or rest longer

Fine ....The end (pronounced "Fee-nay")

Flat sign.............. ♭ ....Lowers a note one half step

Forte .... *f* ....Loud

Fortissimo........... *ff* ....Very loud

Half step ....From one key to the very next key

Legato..Smooth and connected tones, usually indicated by a slur

Mezzo forte .... *mf* ....Moderately loud

Mezzo piano............. *mp* ....Moderately soft

Misterioso..................................In a mysterious manner

Moderato ....A medium rate of speed (not too fast)

Natural sign............ ♮ ....Cancels a sharp or flat

Pianissimo .... *pp* ....Very soft

Piano................. *p* ....Soft

Poco a Poco ....Little by little

Presto ....Very fast

Repeat signs .... :‖ ....Repeat from the beginning

.... ‖: :‖ ....Repeat section between repeat signs

Ritardando ...... *rit., ritard.* ....Gradually slow down

Sforzando .... *sfz* ....Very strong accent

Sharp sign .... ♯ ....Raises a note one half step

Slur .... ⌒ .....A curved line that indicates notes which are to be played legato

Staccato .... ˙ ....Detached, short tones

Tempo ....Rate of speed

Tie .... ⌣ ....A curved line that connects two notes of the same pitch, means to combine their rhythmic values

Trill ....To alternate a note with the next one above, playing one right after the other

Vivace ....Fast and lively

Certificate

of

Achievement

This certifies that

_____

has successfully completed

Grade One of

The Michael Aaron Piano Course

and is now ready to begin

Grade Two

The Michael Aaron Piano Course

_____

Teacher

_____

Date